Lotus Moon

Lotus Moon

The Poetry
of the
Buddhist Nun
Rengetsu

translated and introduced by
John Stevens

White Pine Press • Buffalo, New York

Publication of this book was made possible, in part, with public funds
from the New York State Council on the Arts, a State Agency.

Printed and bound in the United States of America.

First Edition

Library of Congress Control Number: 2005920882

Published by
White Pine Press
P.O. Box 236
Buffalo, New York 14201
www.whitepine.org

Lotus Moon

CONTENTS

INTRODUCTION

John Stevens

Rengetsu was born in the pleasure quarters of Kyoto in
1791, the illegitimate offspring of a high-ranking samurai
and a young geisha. Her natural father arranged for the infant
girl to be adopted by Otagaki Teruhisa, a lay priest serving at
Chionji, head temple of the Pure Land sect of Buddhism.
There Rengetsu learned martial arts, literature, calligraphy,
and the game of *go* under the tutelage of Teruhisa. At the age
of seven or eight she was called to serve as an attendant in the
castle of the lord of Kameoka, a small domain outside Kyoto.
The sprightly young girl continued her classical samurai education at the castle, mastering poetic composition and calligraphy as well as attaining proficiency in the martial arts of

naginata and *jujutsu.* Rengetsu was just as capable of disarming intruders and subduing annoying drunks as she was at making poetry and performing the tea ceremony.

In 1807, the sixteen-year-old beauty was called back to Chionji by Teruhisa and given in marriage a year or so later. Rengetsu enjoyed an enviable childhood, but her early adult years were marked by tragedy. She lost her first child within a month of his birth, her first daughter lived only three years, and a second daughter also died in infancy. Rengetsu then separated from her husband, reportedly because of his dissolute behavior, and he, too, died shortly thereafter.

Rengetsu married again, this time happily, but tragedy struck once more: her second husband fell ill and died while she was pregnant with their second child. Thirty-three years old and twice widowed, she decided to seek refuge from the whirl of *samsara* in religion. In 1824, Rengetsu took orders as a Buddhist nun, and together with Teruhisa and with her two small children, she moved into a small hermitage on the grounds of Chionji. Death continued its relentless assault on Rengetsu's family, however, and by the time she was forty-one her two remaining children and her beloved adoptive father had passed away.

Rengetsu held no official position at Chionji and with Teruhisa gone she was obliged to leave the temple and carry on alone. Since she excelled at the game of *go* she considered becoming a teacher of that demanding art but decided against it—few men cared to admit their inferiority to a woman, and she would have trouble attracting a sufficient number of students. Rengetsu thought of giving lessons in poetry, but that involved self promotion and the securing of patrons, two things a retiring nun wishes to avoid. Finally Rengetsu settled on pottery-making as a means of livelihood. That would allow her to produce something artistic and useful, and perhaps the time-consuming work of pottery-making would serve as a kind of "moving meditation" to assuage the pain in her heart.

Subsequently, the determined forty-one-year-old nun moved to the Okazaki district of Kyoto and learned how to make Shigaraki-style pottery, taking the clay from the hills in Kagura and having her pieces fired at various kilns. Rengetsu's pottery, inscribed with her own poems and paintings, sold well and soon the work of the "beautiful nun in Kyoto" was in demand all over. In fact, the nun was flooded with orders and began moving from place to place to avoid the crush of customers. Rengetsu always kept her few possessions neatly stored in a couple of boxes, ready to change her residence at a moment's notice—in one year alone she moved thirteen times. Part of Rengetsu's inability to settle down is perhaps attributable to the nun's acute sense of life's impermanence— she once likened herself to "a drifting cloud blown by a fierce wind."

Although ordained in the Pure Land School, Rengetsu studied and practiced Zen and Esoteric Buddhism as well, and she was one of those rare Buddhists who successfully integrated all three approaches in her life and work. In her later years the kindly old nun was acclaimed as a patron saint of the arts. Rengetsu was constantly raising money for the relief of disaster victims and more than once gave away, on the spot, her outer kimono to beggars she found wandering on the street. One night a misdirected thief entered her little hut and the frugal-living nun held a light for him to see better: "You won't find anything of value here but you are welcome to whatever you need. You must be starving to be so desperate. Let me fix you a bowl of tea-rice."

Since Rengetsu's pottery was so popular—it is said that at one time every household in Kyoto had at least a few pieces of Rengetsu-*yaki*—a number of other kilns began turning out imitations. One such kiln had the audacity to ask Rengetsu to inscribe the fakes because, "although the pottery is not hard to duplicate, your calligraphy is inimitable!" The unworldly nun not only agreed to do so, but also gave the kiln a few genuine pieces to help them do a better job of copying her.

The charitable Rengetsu similarly assisted struggling young artists by inscribing her poems on their works, thus making them easier to sell. Rengetsu wrote a number of poems on sheets of paper for the future use of Tomioka Tessai (1837–1924): "When times are hard, add your paintings to these sheets and sell them." (Tessai eventually emerged as Japan's foremost modern *nanga* painter.)

Rengetsu was a celebrity in the cultural life of the ancient capital of Kyoto, acquainted with most of the literary and artistic luminaries of her time, as well as the statesmen who spearheaded the Meiji Restoration of 1868. Like most

Kyotoites, Rengetsu was an ardent supporter of the Emperor, believing that the restoration of imperial rule would usher in a golden age of learning and culture, but she also pleaded with both sides involved in the conflict to refrain from bloodshed. Incidentally, Rengetsu was offended by the arrogant "open the country or else" threat of the American Commodore Perry, and wrote a poem encouraging the men and women of Japan not to be cowed by such brute force.

Regarding poetry, Rengetsu was greatly influenced by the theories of Ozawa Roan (1723–1801) and Kagawa Kageki (1768–1843), both of whom emphasized direct, simple expression of genuine feelings rather than rhetorical flourish in the composition of verse; poems should utilize everyday language and natural human emotions. Thus Rengetsu's poetry—all in the form of *waka,* classical verse in a 5-7-5-7-7 syllable pattern—celebrates the things around her and the emotions she experienced in her daily life as an artist, as a Buddhist practitioner, and as an emancipated woman.

In the realm of calligraphy, the art which has won her the widest appreciation, Rengetsu seems not to have studied any one style in particular. Her unique brushwork developed naturally, and it is extremely elegant and refined. Free-flowing, yet perfectly controlled and centered, Rengetsu's calligraphy is distinctively feminine, while strong and supple enough to be the envy of even the most forceful male calligraphers.

Rengetsu remained productive until the very end of her life, producing upwards of fifty thousand pieces of art— including her pottery, hundreds of paintings, and thousands of poemcards. She died peacefully at the age of eighty-four on December 10, 1875 in the tea room of Jinkoin Temple.

THE POEMS

Two collections of Rengetsu's verse were published in her lifetime. *Rengetsu Shikibu nijo waka shu* (Poems by Rengetsu and Shikibu), with forty-nine *waka* by Rengetsu and fifty-six by Takabatake Shikibu (1785-1881), appeared in 1868. *Ama no karumo* (A Diver's Harvest of Seaweed), containing about three-hundred *waka* by Rengetsu alone, was printed in 1870. *Rengetsuni zenshu* (The Complete Works of the Nun Rengetsu) lists approximately nine-hundred *waka*, with about six hundred in various collections and another three hundred or so scattered throughout her letters and notebooks. The selection of *waka* presented here follows the traditional format: poems are grouped according to subject matter in a sequence that runs through the four seasons, beginning in spring, and ends with a gathering of miscellaneous poems.

Japanese poetry in general, and Rengetsu's verse in particular, tends to be understated and evocative, leaving it to the reader to fill in and flesh out that which is alluded to in the words and phrases of the poems. A reader of *waka* is also expected to augment the sentiments expressed in a poem with his or her own experiences. Rengetsu's poems impart to us a keen sense of her time and place, and her life a Buddhist nun and artist, while speaking to us of emotions, sensations, and truths that are universally valid.

Spring

MOUNTAIN RETREAT

Living deep in the mountains
I've grown fond of the
Solitary sound of the singing pines;
On days the wind does not blow,
How lonely it is!

Spring Moon

In the moonlight
Of early spring,
Lingering snow
Bids farewell to a village
Yearning for its first flower.

Tender Buds

A thousand grasses
Run rampant in autumn
But to discover a
Single sprout with two leaves:
The joy of spring!

Spring Sunrise

Dawn today—
High above the river,
Mountains thick-set with snow;
Down below,
The roar of the flowing water.

SPRING ICE

The thick river ice
Begins to break,
The mountain well, too,
Starts to thaw
Allowing me to scoop up spring.

Spring ice,
In the valley river
Mirrors
The flight of bush-warblers
Hurrying to the capital.

PLUM BLOSSOMS

Eagerly awaiting
The bush-warblers:
The lovely plum trees
Along my garden wall
Burst into bloom.

In Japanese art and poetry, bush-warblers (uguisu) are always paried with plum blossoms. A plum tree, the first plant to flower in the spring, is a symbol of endurance and renewal; the bush-warbler, a tiny bird of great beauty, breaks into song at the coming of the new season. (The bird's cry sounds like "*hokke-kyo,*" the Japanese for *Lotus Sutra.*)

A Day the Plum Trees Near My Hermitage Were In Bloom

When the bush-warblers
Come to the capital
I'd like to lend them
My little hut—
Plum flowers in full bloom.

UPON HEARING THE FIRST BUSH-WARBLER OF SPRING

Amid the plum blossoms,
I hear the first burst of song;
Too young yet to give a
Full-throated performance,
Still, what a joy!

Evening Plum Blossoms

As the night advances
The fragrance of the blossoms
Perfumes both the
Sleeves of my black robe
And the recesses of my heart.

Returning Geese

The fragrance of plum blossoms
All around my pillow—
Night deepens,
Returning spring geese
Honk high above.

SWALLOWS

Near the eaves of my hut,
Swallows,
Coming and going,
Hurrying to the nest,
No time to rest.

VIOLETS

From Kasuga Field,
That ancient place,
These little purple flowers,
A reminder of the
Violets of old.

Spring Rain

Random thoughts
And loneliness trouble me
But I am soothed by the
Anticipation of cherry blossoms
And spring rain falling on my hut.

March Third

As an offering today
To this lord and lady:
Freshly opened peach blossoms.
The joy of countless springs
Is once again ours.

Upon Hearing the Bells at Yoshimizu

The echo of the bell
At Yoshimizu—
I am here, too,
In a black robe
Set against the white mist.

Yoshimizu is a spot in Kyoto's Higashiyama district noted for its scenery.

MIST

From morning,
Perfectly tranquil,
Far removed from
The world's turmoil—
One with the spring mist.

SPRING WIND

Eternal spring wind,
I know you won't be too rough
On the delicate
Branches and buds
Of the weeping willow.

The Willow at the Window

So quickly!
The willow planted
Three years ago
Now beating against
My windowpane.

Cherry Blossoms

Even though I want
To come again tomorrow,
I'll take a branch of
Mountain blossoms
To keep me company.

SHRINE BLOSSOMS

At the shrine of
Imperial princesses,
Spring purification rites are performed
As cherry blossoms mingle with
The leaves of the sacred sakaki tree.

In old Japan, there were shrines where imperial priestesses secluded them-selves to perform purification rites. The cherry blossoms are the Buddhist flower of impermanence; the *sakaki,* is the sacred tree of Shinto.

A Trip During
Cherry Blossom Season

No place at the inn
But I find consolation
Sleeping beneath the
Hazy moon and the
Cherry blossoms.

Mountain Falling Flowers

We accept the graceful falling
Of mountain cherry blossoms,
But it is much harder for us
To fall away from our own
Attachment to the world.

Falling Flowers at an Ancient Temple

Now spring is complete—
A mountain breeze
Catches up the
Remaining blossoms in
Billowing white clouds.

The Butterfly

Fluttering about sleepily
In a field of
Dew-kissed flowers—
Could it be the little butterfly
Of Chuang-t'zu's dream

This refers to the famous tale of the Taoist philosopher Chuang-t'zu awakening from a nap to wonder: "Am I a man dreaming I am a butterfly or a butterfly dreaming I am a man?"

FROG

As I reach to gather
Some fallen blossoms
A frog leaps into the stream
And then floats about
The water in protest.

Summer

EARLY SUMMER WATER

The blossoms have fallen,
The fetters of my heart
Have also loosened,
And it has become summer:
A rivulet murmurs cool and clear.

CHANGE OF GARMENTS

I'll be changing into
My summer robes today
But my heart is
Still stained with
The color of spring blossoms.

EARLY SUMMER BREEZES

Abundant clouds,
A few lingering blossoms,
Fresh summer mountains,
Fragrant green leaves,
And gentle cool breezes.

First Cry of the Cuckoo

When will it sing?
In this ancient village,
The cuckoo
Conceals itself
Until the sixth month.

CUCKOO IN THE FOREST

The night lingers—
In the lovely forest
The voice of the cuckoo
Cloaked in green leaves
And mist . . .

"Cuckoo" *(hototogisu)* is a key "season word" for summer in Japanese poetry.

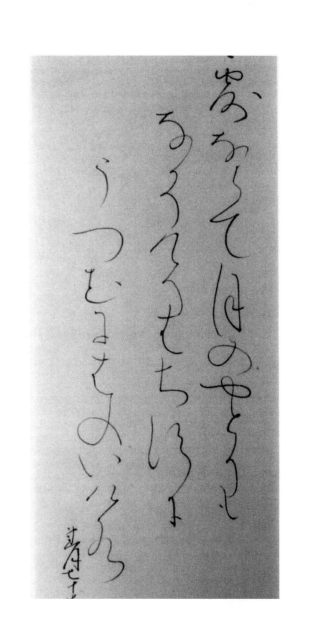

PASSING BY MT. SHIGA AFTER
ATTENDING THE SANNO FESTIVAL

An early morning gust of wind
Has broken the bramble flowers:
A cuckoo sings
This June,
Here on Mt. Shiga.

Shiga is a mountain on the outskirts of Kyoto. Rengetsu often visited the place with her second husband prior to his death. The Sanno Shrine Festival, one of the year's major events in Kyoto, is held on nearby Mt. Hiei.

In the Vicinity of Mt. Kase

Still light—
The cuckoo's song
Here on Kase
Will be my souvenir tomorrow
When I return to the capital.

Mt. Kase is located south of Kyoto on the way to Nara.

ANCIENT VILLA FLOWERS

The single memento of
A once great family:
Little sunflowers
Along the fence
Of the abandoned villa.

EVENING COOL BY THE SEA

Cooling off in a boat
That sways as if drunk—
In the bay breeze
The moon on the waves
Seems a bit tipsy too!

MOON IN THE SUMMER TREES

What a delight—
Leaves hide my little hut
From the hot sun by day;
At night, moonlight
Filters through the trees.

SUMMER MOON

The cool shadow
Of the bright moon
In an open field
Makes you forget
All daytime worries.

Mosquito Smudge

Seaside village:
Mosquito smudge smolders
Throughout the cool evening,
But the thin smoke leaves
The moon untouched.

Bamboo

This gentleman
grows and grows
Auspiciously:
Learn from it and
You will ever flourish.

CORMORANT RIVER FIREFLIES

The flitting fireflies:
Willingly sacrificing
Themselves
To the torches
On Cormorant River.

In old Japan, cormorants—bound around the neck to prevent them from swallowing—were used to catch river fish at night. The fish were attracted to torches hung from the sides of the boats.

LOTUS FLOWER

If I, too, could somehow
Open the lotus blossom
Within my own heart
And color it pure white
How happy I would be . . .

CICADAS

No light yet,
Night lingers on,
But already from the tops
Of the trees hiding my hut
Cicadas shriek.

BATS IN THE MOONLIGHT

In the pale moonlight,
Near the eaves of my hut,
Fluttering about the
Swaying willow branches,
My old friends—little bats!

Rainy Season

A steady sprinkle,
No sight of the sun,
Day after day,
Forests swallowed by clouds:
Fifth month rains.

In Japan, there is a distinct fifth season of cloudy skies and frequent rain. According to the old calendar this season was called "Fifth month rains"; today the season is referred to as *tsuyu or baiyu*, and it usually runs from late May or early June

MOONFLOWERS

The silver crescent
Shines dimly
But the night is
Brightened up by
The moonflowers.

Autumn

Autumn Retreat

Deep in the mountains
A single branch of maple
Near the eaves of my hut
Marks the beginning
Of the days of autumn.

Enjoying an Autumn Evening

In the fields, in the mountains
I was enthralled, so enthralled;
On the way back home,
The autumn moon accompanied me
Right to my room.

An Immortal's Elixir

Chrysanthemum dew:
Lift it up,
Take a big sip,
And you will be immortal,
Not aging, not dying!

Taoist immortals are said to maintain their longevity by "feasting on dew."

MUMBLING TO MYSELF ON SEPTEMBER NINTH

Picking chrysanthemums,
Hoping to recapture my youth:
My old body, however, has piled up
More years than this
Growing mound of flowers!

September 9 is considered the peak of the chrysanthemum season, and an ancient Chinese legend has it that if one gathers flowers on this day and prepares a concoction of the petal, one's life will be greatly lengthened.

Gazing at the Moon
Night after Night

The autumn moon—
It, too,
Can become
A tie to
Floating world.

The autumn moon, a symbol of enlightenment, is often an object of contemplation for Buddhists.

As a Nun, Gazing at the Deep Colors of Autumn

Clad in black robes
I should have no attractions to
The shapes and scents of this world
But how can I keep my vows
Gazing at today's crimson maple leaves?

Autumn Night

This autumn night,
Dozing and dreaming
Of this sorry world,
Then startled by the
Temple bell at daybreak.

Morning Glories

In a gap
Between the clouds:
Faint moonbeams
Reach down on grass tangled
With morning glories.

A Visit to Tagano-o to View the Crimson Maple Leaves

I cannot leave without
Breaking off a branch of a
Tagano-o autumn maple—
If a few leaves happen to fall
Please forgive me, mountain guardians!

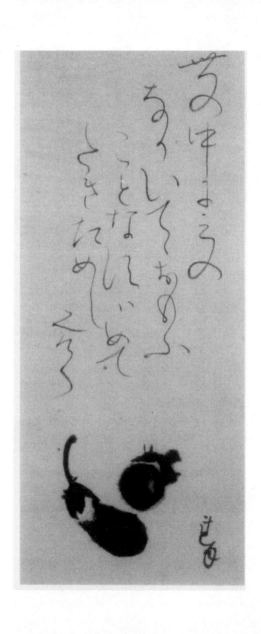

LIVING NEAR THE GREAT BUDDHA

My night: autumn chill,
A steady drizzle
Of cold rain, and
The flicker of
Lonely shadows.

The Great Buddha is housed in the colossal main hall of the remple
Todaiji in Nara.

CHESTNUTS

Amid the
Crimson maples
Mountain chestnuts
Ripe with burrs:
The munificence of autumn!

MOUNTAIN VILLAGE FOG

Overgrown kudzu vines,
Not a visitor for ages;
Along the hedge
Autumn fog wells up
In the mountain village.

Field of Wild Flowers

Rather than cutting them down
To spread out or gather up,
Let the wild flowers of autumn be
And enjoy the field
Just as it is . . .

Autumn Rain

The sun sets,
And the shadows deepen
Around the pines of Irie—
Lonely memories
In the autumn rain.

Irie is the old name for the area around Chionji, Rengetsu's home temple.

SEASHORE MOON

I walk along Akashi Bay
This moonlit autumn evening
Trying to pick up
Words beautiful enough
To capture the scene.

Akashi Bay is one of Japan's famed scenic spots.

In Autumn I visited a mountain temple. The wild bushclover mingled with the flowering pampas grass along the hedge, and various insects sang in unison. When the moment captivates you . . .

> Perfectly aware,
> Not a thought,
> Just the moon
> Piercing me with light
> As I gaze upon it.

INSECTS CHIRPING IN THE MOONLIGHT

From a crack in the wall
Of my mountain hut:
Katydids announce themselves
And moonlight too
pours in.

Insects in the Moonlight

In the pure moonlight
A chorus of insects
Chirp along the hedge:
The cold, too, deepens
As the night lengthens.

Autumn Tears

In the sky,
Flocks of departing geese;
In the weeds,
Murmuring insects—
Tears like dew well up in my eyes.

INSECTS AT A SHRINE

Autumn harmony:
Wind in the pines,
Bell cricket melodies,
A country shrine
Hung with sacred festoons.

THE PLEASURES OF AN AUTUMN EVENING

On each dewdrop,
I count one
Moon after another,
All night
To daybreak.

Autumn Paddies

Pouring rain,
Evening gloom,
In the mountain paddies:
Other than a scarecrow,
Not a soul around . . .

POUNDING CLOTH

The night lengthens
As I pound and pound
My worn nun's robe;
The hour grows later and later—
Autumn here in Shino Village.

In old Japan, cloth was pounded to remove the dirt and improve the gloss.

Winter

EARLY WINTER

On the treetop
A few wild persimmons
Have yet to fall—
The color of
Autumn lingers in my eyes.

FROST

As the moon ascends,
Plovers cry along
The Kamo River—
Night deepens, first frost
Settles on my sleeves.

SHUT UP IN FALLING LEAVES

The pile of
Fallen leaves
Separates my hermitage
Further and further
From the world of woe.

WINTER CONFINEMENT IN
SHIGARAKI VILLAGE

Last night's storm was fierce,
As I can see by this morning's
Thick blanket of snow:
Rising to kindle woodchips,
In lonely Shigaraki Village.

Rengetsu often went to Shigaraki Village to dig clay for her pottery.

A DAY OF HAIL

Will the paper on
My makeshift
Little window
Withstand the assault
Of the hailstones?

MOUNTAIN RETREAT IN WINTER

The little persimmons drying outside
Under the eaves
Of my hermitage—
Are they freezing tonight
In the winter storm?

STORM

The pine tree
That provides my shade
Is driven down
Against my window
By the raging storm.

SEASHORE SNOW

The sea breeze
Gradually calms
As the night lengthens
And lustrous white snow
Piles up on the pines of Naruo.

The seashore at Naruo is noted for its splendid pines.

COLD NIGHT

The frigid north wind
Blows through the spaces of
My tattered window screen;
The cold blast keeps both the screen
And my eyes open all night.

WINTER DREAMS

To forget the chill of
The frozen hearth
I spend the night
Dreaming of gathering
Violets in a lush field.

COLD RAIN AT THE SEASHORE

Looking out over the bay,
I see clouds of cold rain
Summoning winter,
And hear the wind in the pines
Whisper its name.

ICE IN THE MOUNTAIN WELL

Yesterday,
I shattered the ice
To draw water—
No matter, this morning
Frozen just as solid.

Removing the Soot

Clearing the soot
From the beams,
Sweeping the dust
From my hearth,
Getting ready for the New Year.

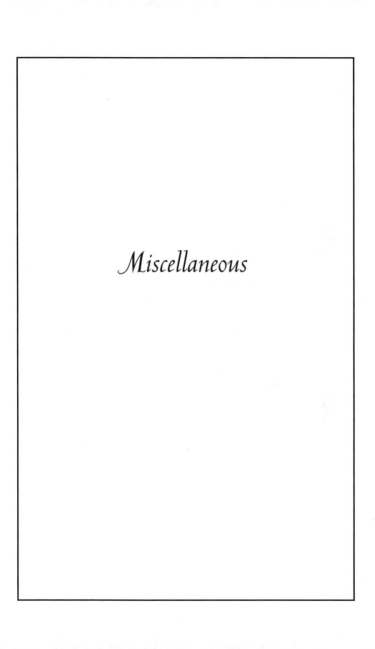

Miscellaneous

ALONG THE UJI RIVER, RECALLING THE PAST

Here the brave samurai
Of old once
Forded this river—
Their names now borne away
Forever by the water of the Uji.

River

This floating world's
Dust and dirt
Flows away
And all is purified
By the waves of the Kamo River

The Kamo River, once famed for its fast-flowing pure water, runs through
the center of Kyoto.

AT SAKURAI VILLAGE

To my beloved child(ren),
My final message:
Flowers blooming
With all their heart
In lovely Sakurai Village.

This refers to the parting of the warrior Kusunoki Masashige (d. 1336)
and his son Masatsura that took place in Sakurai. Masashige knew that
he would not return alive from the fateful battle of Minatogawa, and bid
his son farewell, comparing the life of a samurai to the cherry blossoms,
glorious but short-lived. It is likely that Rengetsu is also alluding to her
own dead children.

Working in the North Mountains

From dawn to dusk,
Spending the day
Gathering clay:
Surely Buddha would not
Think this a trifling matter.

BLACKENED THING

Another year passes:
On my kitchen shelf
Something blackened
With soot—
A little Buddha image.

Seeing Young Nuns on Their Begging Rounds

First steps on the
Long path to Truth:
Please do not dream
Your lives away,
Walk on to the end.

WHEN PEOPLE TEASE ME ABOUT MY CONSTANT CHANGE OF RESIDENCE

A floating cloud,
Drifting about
Playfully
Here and there
Not wanting to fade away.

THE ONI

Do not resist, (Mr. Oni):
Open the lotus inside
And overturn
All those demons
In your heart!

Oni are ferocious little goblins that sometimes can be converted to Buddhism, transforming their demonic power into a force for good.

HEART

Coming and going,
Without beginning or end,
Like ever changing
White clouds:
The heart of things.

The Pleasures of Calligraphy

Taking up the brush
Just for the joy of it,
Writing on and on,
Leaving behind
Long lines of dancing letters.

INCENSE BURNER

A single line of
Fragrant smoke
From the incense stick
Trails off without a trace:
One's heart, as well?

A Life of Retirement

Reside in a living landscape
And it becomes yours:
Daikon dry along the fence,
Trees full of chestnuts
Brush against the eaves.

Daikon are giant white radishes that can be eaten raw, boiled, or pickled.

THOUGHTS WHILE MAKING
A FLOWER POT

Dew and butterflies are
Attracted to flowers of
Certain scent and color:
Do they have
favorites too?

Digging Clay and Making a Vase

Taking the fragile
Little handmade
Thing to sell—
How lonely it looks
In the market place!

TRAVELERS AT NIGHT

Their way lit
By pine torches,
Swords firmly set,
Warriors head resolutely
Towards Saya-no-Nakayama.

In the old days, provincial lords were obliged to spend every other year in attendance on the shogun in Edo, and colorful processions of traveling samurai were a common sight along the highways. Saya-no-Nakayama in Shizuoka was an important way-station .

MOUNTAIN RETREAT

The roar of the waterfall,
The howl of a
Mountain storm—
Will they shout out to me
Until morning?

STORM DEEP IN THE MOUNTAINS

The roar awakens me from
A peaceful slumber
But then the fierce
Mountain wind blows away
All the dust in my heart.

On the Fighting During the Restoration

To those who strike,
And those who are struck,
Keep this in your hearts:
Are we not all people
Of the same wonderful land?

As the Tokugawa shogunate tottered toward collapse in the 1860s, fierce fighting broke out in Japan, culminating in rhe Meiji Restoration of 1868.

INSCRIPTION PLACED ON A PAINTING OF A COURTESAN

Spring and fall,
Playing and playing:
Faint memories
Of days in old places
So long ago.

My Thoughts

Someday I, too,
Will be crossing over:
In tonight's dreams,
A floating dream bridge
To the other shore.

Moon Over the Bridge

Spanning the known
And unknown past,
Bearing all the pathos
The world offers:
Moonlit Uji Bridge

Uji Bridge is the sight of many important events and battles in Japanese history.

SPEAR BEARER

Swaggering along
Intent on serving his lord
The spearbearer moves ahead
Hoping to impress all
The people of Asuka Pass.

Spearbearers were the vanguards of the spectacular processions that provincial lords were obliged to make to and from the shogun's capital of Edo. The spearbearers, brandishing long lances topped with feathers and animal fur, swaggered from side to side, lifting their legs high up into the air to attract attention.

Fisherman Singing to the Moon

Rhythmically he poles
In time to the music
Of his folk song:
A fisherman's little boat
Drenched in moonlight.

Humble in Body But Pure in Heart

Bodies bent and shaky,
But mountain folk
Always keep their
Minds as polished
As their sickles.

DHARMA LIGHT

If you want to
Extend the light
Of the Dharma,
Let it first illumine
Your own heart.

"Dharma" is a synonym for "the teachings of Buddhism."

WHEN A THIEF CAME

If the mountain bandit
Came to my place
To steal away
Golden oak leaves
He struck it rich!

THE THIEF

Not a trace
Of the thief
But he left behind
The peaceful stillness
Of the Okazaki Hills.

LIVING IN A HERMITAGE AMONG THE PINES

Before setting out again
On another bumpy sojourn
In this floating world
I settle for a while
In the shade of the pines.

SAKE

Enjoy delicious sake
Without overdoing it
And it becomes
An elixir that eases
Old age and death.

むさし

麁ものまに

うれ、るい

ひをもて

ひしち

ちうの

喜

THIRTY YEARS AFTER
MY HUSKAND'S DEATH

The evanescence of
This floating world
I feel over and over:
It is hardest
To be the one left behind.

MEMORIES OF MY HUSBAND

Together we enjoyed
The cherry blossoms,
And passed long summers
In the mountains:
Standing here, such sadness.

Death Verse

How I hope to pass away
While gazing at a round moon
In a cloudless sky that
Shines over lotus flowers
In full bloom.

In her late seventies, Rengetsu prepared a casket for her funeral. Inside she placed a nun's hat and a white shroud which had on it a painting of a moon and a lotus by Tessai. Between these two symbols of enlightenment and purity, Rengetsu wrote this death verse.

Afterword: Hermitage Heart

Bonnie Myotai Treace, *Sensei*

A scent of woodsmoke and incense, wind wrapping itself around a small hut, the quiet presence of a settled, generous spiritual friend: to sit with the poems of the Buddhist nun Rengetsu is to allow a teacher into the depth of one's mind. Over the winter, this has been my practice, taking up a few of Rengetsu's winter-inspired *waka* verses and staying with them, committing myself to let them inform whatever teaching happens during this time.

Keeping that commitment hasn't always been easy. Some of Rengetsu's writing is so strong that it is immediately engaging, and stirs that sense of trust and humility which comes so naturally when excellence takes hold of one's attention. Nothing truer or finer beckons; restlessness slips away. But some of her verses, like many of the classic koans in the collections used in Zen training, lie a little flat initially and take more work to open up. Since commitment to any practice means not moving to something easier when it gets difficult, the challenge has been to stay with them and give even her harder-to-appreciate poems time to work on the heart and soften the impulse to reject them and move on.

Rengetsu lived what could have easily become a tragic life. She was born the daughter of a courtesan and a samurai, but her natural father had her adopted by a lay priest serving at

Chionji, Japan's head temple of the Pure Land sect of Buddhism. Her adopted father, Teruhisa, seems to have been devoted to Rengetsu. He taught her martial arts, calligraphy, and an appreciation for art and literature which later—in a certain way—would save her life. For several years she served as an attendant to the lord of Kameoka, a city near Kyoto, and was fortunate in being able to continue her classical education while there.

But then the challenges began to roll in: she was married off, had three children who died in early infancy, and separated from a husband who abused her, and who also died shortly thereafter. She married again, and while she was pregnant with their second child, her husband became ill and passed away. Try to imagine, if you will, this woman's life: thirty-three years old, with two small children, and having experienced more heartbreak and loss than most of us will know in a lifetime. If ever there was an excuse for feeling overwhelmed and depressed, her life certainly offered one.

One pleasure of discovering the lives and teachings of the rare women we find in the history of Buddhism is seeing how they take up the tragedies in their lives and transform them. They remind us of the freedom that no circumstance can take from us. Because their stories are generally less accessible —and because the luxury of serious religious training was less available to them—finding someone like Rengetsu is a great gift. She faced this moment in her life when despair could have taken hold, when impermanence had pretty much whipped her to the bone, and somehow her heart sparked.

She ordained, taking her children with her to live on the grounds of Chionji with Teruhisa, and practiced in earnest. Still, death kept coming, and by the time she was forty-one, her remaining children and the adoptive father she had loved since childhood all were gone. Not allowed to remain at Chionji, she then had to find her way alone.

She walked into a world that attempted to limit her on the basis of her gender. It's said she considered whether she could make a living as a teacher of the game go, at which she excelled, but recognized that few male students would be able to muster student-mind with a woman teacher. She soon realized that art would be her path, and began making pottery as a kind of moving meditation, inscribing each piece with a bit of poetry.

Over time her work became immensely popular, so much so that she found it necessary to never stay long in any one place, or crowds would begin to gather around her. Likening herself to a "drifting cloud," she was still incredibly prolific, with her work becoming one of the most generous, sustained offerings of deep spiritual practice in Buddhist history. Reputedly, she was able to raise large sums of money for disaster victims because of her ability to be as at ease intermingling with the statesmen and great artists of her day, as she was meditating or making pottery alone in her hut. When she died in 1875 at the age of eighty-four, she left a legacy of more than fifty thousand pieces of pottery, calligraphy, paintings, and poetry. She is remembered not as a tragic figure, but as one of those rare human beings who drew from a seemingly bottomless well of strength and love.

The three Rengetsu winter poems that I'd like to introduce to you today have a straightforward, unadorned quality, as does most of her writing. And although she did not organize them into the sequence in which they appear in Stevens' book, their progression struck me as — however inadvertently—expressing a spiritual journey itself.

I'd recently advised a friend of mine who was stymied on a writing project to try the device that novel writers sometimes use to provide a frame for their stories ("Chapter One... In which a man goes in search of a whale..."). I decided to give my own advice a try: "Three Poems of Rengetsu ... in which a spiritual journey is indicated, though never baldly named... in which what is subtle and intuitive is immediate and uncomplicated... in which what is interior and private is also the exterior condition, the public expression...."

Winter Confinement in Shigaraki Village

Last night's storm was fierce
As I can see by this morning's
Thick blanket of snow
Rising to kindle wood chips
In lonely Shigaraki Village.

Shigaraki Village is where Rengetsu would go to get the clay for her pottery. This is such a beautifully simple poem —

a woman enters a hut, she's come some distance, she's worked all day. Darkness comes. At dawn, she sees snow blanketing the hills and knows that there must have been a fierce storm in the night. She kindles the fire. In its thusness, it is just thus.

But as we stay with the poem, we might find ourselves reflecting on the journey we make to find the clay for our own vessel. We might begin to wonder about leaving home and coming to dwell alone. During our ango at the temple, each of us, for instance, is asked to leave our familiar patterns and intensify practice: to dwell peacefully in each moment's sufficiency, making our home there. When monastics ordain, it's the same deal; we become unsui, "clouds and water," letting go of the activities in our life that are self-securing, and giving ourselves to the journey that is itself our home. So, when the poet makes her pilgrimage to Shigaraki, to go with her is to take that journey as well. Will we go, gather the clay for our real work, and settle into the moment?

In Shigaraki village, the poet is waking up. She's inferring from the evidence the realities of a night's storm. It's interesting that in the Buddhist tradition, night is often used to point to total intimacy, the reality of oneness, of not separating the self from things. In the night, or "darkness," there is no distinction, no separation between seer and seen. In the words of the Heart Sutra, it is the time of "no eye, ear, nose, tongue, body, mind." What is that night? Of course, when many of us begin to sense the "fierce storm" of night in spiritual life, we may yearn for nothing but to be elsewhere. On the edge of it, we pull back, trying to hold onto something of ourselves.

Haven't you felt that resistance that thrives right on the cusp of breaking through? There, on the edge, most of us have some kind of argument. "I can't sit another minute," we say. Or, "I can't see this koan." Or, "I don't know how to love this person." The poem points to a kind of sweet constancy, the kindling of the fire. Just take care of the moment. Stoke the flame when it falters. The poet stirs the wood chips; we stir our life to find the warm center of things. What is that center?

Master Dogen writes, "When the Dharma does not fill your whole body and mind, you think it's already sufficient. When the Dharma fills your body and mind, you understand something is missing." What is needed? The world has never depended more than it does now on those who will genuinely ask that question. Always encourage each other to go deeply into that inquiry. How might you serve? What remains to be seen?

Dogen continues, "To study the Buddha way is to study the self. To study the self is to forget the self. To forget the self is to be confirmed by the ten thousand things. To be confirmed by the ten thousand things is to cast off body and mind of self as well as that of others. No trace of realization remains, and this no trace is continued endlessly."

The fire of our freedom will always warm the hut, but somehow we won't feel it unless we kindle it. And that kindling of the fire continues. It's not on the clock, like a workday we can't wait to see end. It's loving, and essentially timeless. Practically, getting this point means we're relieved of feeling we're behind or progressing too slowly in our training, or that we're spiritually talented and should set our sights on becoming teachers. It's just time to kindle the woodchips and get over yourself.

In the hut where she's come to make the vessel, responsible for the fire, awake to the night's storm as it was revealed only in the the light, the poet then faces the day. Our second poem:

A Day of Hail

Will the paper
On my makeshift
Little window
Withstand the assault
Of the hailstones?

A poem in which a woman, alone in a hut, wonders if her small window made of fragile paper will be strong enough not to be ripped apart by a long day of pelting hail. Simple enough: the sound of heavy stones of solid water hitting and hitting and hitting, the paper window pocking with each hit, quivering, providing such a thin barrier against the storm.

What is this makeshift window — this temporary point of view, if you will? The poet takes us into a day in which the essential vulnerability of our position is a visceral reality. She invites us to feel and hear and taste the aliveness of right now.

How do we live with impermanence? By adding another layer to the window? By praying for sunnier days? We cannot stop the hail, Rengetsu seems to whisper, but we can be awake. Awake and at peace.

How do you find that peace?

Be yourself. Be yourself, and live that boundless reality intimately, generously, freely. Usually, if you ask someone who they are, you're likely to get the list: "I went to this college, I'm married to this person, I know how to make soup, I'm good at this, I'm bad at that, I can do this, I can do that." We list all the aggregates, all the things that change, all the makeshift identities. But what is the real nature of the self? Noticing the thinness of the seeming barrier between inside and out, just experience that permeability. What are we protecting?

A monk asked Master Tozan, "When cold and heat come, how can we avoid them?" How do we live in this world of trouble, of suffering, of horror, of change, where we can't hold onto what's pleasant or completely get away from what's unpleasant? How can we avoid the heat and cold? Tozan replied, "Go to where there is no heat or cold."

The monk then implored, "But how do I get to that place where there is no heat or cold?" Tozan said, "When it's cold, the cold kills you. When it's hot, the heat kills you." In other words, kill the separation. Quit living in fear of what might be, and dwell in this.

But what about the assault of the hailstones? When what hits is not just weather but something that arrives with intent to harm, what then? I find it inspiring that Rengetsu spends none of the precious moments in her poem cursing the sky, or dissecting the cause of precipitation.

Why are so many people trying to kill so many people? Why is there such enormous greed? Why is there evil? Why did this happen to me? We should consider how a day of hail might be simply, utterly that: a day of hail. Not to be denied, not feared, not hidden from. There's a story told about an old fisherman out on a very foggy day. Suddenly, this other boat comes and crashes into him. He spends the next couple of hours battening down the boat where it's leaking and cursing this sailor who shouldn't even be on the water, ruined his day, ruined his catch, ruined his family's meal, and his livelihood. Enraged, he works through the morning, cussing and cursing as, gradually, the fog begins to lift.

Suddenly he sees that what hit him wasn't another boat — it was a rock. All at once, he regretted the hours wasted in such anger, the birds he didn't hear, the enjoyment he didn't feel.

Mountain Retreat in Winter

> The little persimmons drying outside
> Under the eaves
> Of my hermitage
> Are they freezing tonight
> In the winter storm?

This last of our three poems brings us into the hermitage again, with a feeling of the life under its eaves. Entering it, in a sense we enter the heart of Buddhism. We stop waiting for company. We stop needing others to show us what's normal, to know what we should do. We sit alone. That's the first teaching gesture of the Buddha: he stopped deferring and referring and looking for an authority. He just sat down — in his own life, in his own mind, in his own condition, with his own karma — and aloneness was transformed. The whole world wasn't excluded; when he sat, the dividing wall between his life, mind, condition and karma and that of the world was dropped. This is the hermitage heart that beats in each of us. We just need to stop being too afraid to trust it.

Practice is the journey to that trust. It begins when we stop waiting for someone to say: here's the plan, here's the right thing to do, here's the act of courage, of attention, of kindness, of wisdom that you can make. Each of us has that wisdom. Each of us, in fact, is that wisdom. Each of us can leap thoroughly into that hermitage heart and get on with it. We don't need another life, a different condition, a greater wisdom, a better personality. We just need to take care of the life under the eaves of this measureless hermitage.

How? In asking, we begin the journey home.

Bonnie Myotai Treace, Sensei is Daido Roshi's senior Dharma successor. She serves as Vice-Abbess of ZMM and Spiritual Director of Zen Center of New York City.

Companions for the Journey Series

This series presents inspirational work by well-known writers
in a small-book format designed to be carried along
on your journey through life.

Volume 7
Lotus Moon
The Poetry of Rengetsu
Translated by John Stevens
Afterword by Bonnie Myotai Treace
1-893996-36-0   5 x 7   132 pages $14.00

Volume 6
A Zen Forest: Zen Sayings
Translated by Soioku Shigematsu
Preface by Gary Snyder
1-893996-30-1   5 x 7   140 pages $14.00

Volume 5
Back Roads to Far Towns
Basho's Travel Journal
Translated by Cid Corman
1-893996-31-X   5 x 7   128 pages $13.00

Volume 4
Heaven My Blanket, Earth My Pillow
Poems from Sung Dynasty China by Yang Wan-Li
Translated by Jonathan Chaves
1-893996-29-8   5 x 7   120 pages $14.00

Volume 3
10,000 Dawns
The Love Poems of Claire and Yvan Goll
Translated by Thomas Rain Crowe and Nan Watkins
I-893996-27-I   5 x 7   96 pages $13.00

Volume 2
There Is No Road
Proverbs by Antonio Machado
Translated by Mary G. Berg & Dennis Maloney
I-893996-66-2   5 x 7   120 pages $14.00

Volume I
Wild Ways: Zen Poems of Ikkyu
Translated by John Stevens
I-893996-65-4   5 x 7   128 pages $14.00